Science In Your Life:
ENERGY
GET MOVING!

Wendy Sadler

www.raintreepublishers.co.uk

Visit our website to find out more information about **Raintree** books.

To order:
- ☎ Phone 44 (0) 1865 888112
- 🖹 Send a fax to 44 (0) 1865 314091
- 💻 Visit the Raintree bookshop at **www.raintreepublishers.co.uk** to browse our catalogue and order online.

First published in Great Britain by Raintree, Halley Court, Jordan Hill, Oxford OX2 8EJ, part of Harcourt Education.
Raintree is a registered trademark of Harcourt Education Ltd.

© Harcourt Education Ltd 2006
First published in paperback in 2007
The moral right of the proprietor has been asserted.

Editorial: Melanie Copland, Kate Buckingham, and Lucy Beevor
Design: Victoria Bevan and Bridge Creative Services Ltd
Picture Research: Hannah Taylor and Catherine Bevan
Production: Duncan Gilbert

Originated by Chroma Graphics (Overseas) Pte. Ltd
Printed and bound in China by South China Printing Company

10 digit ISBN 1 844 43662 4 (hardback)
13 digit ISBN 978 1 844 43662 0 (hardback)
10 09 08 07 06 05
10 9 8 7 6 5 4 3 2 1

10 digit ISBN 1 844 43680 2 (paperback)
13 digit ISBN 978 1 844 43680 4 (paperback)
11 10 09 08 07 06
10 9 8 7 6 5 4 3 2 1

British Library Cataloguing in Publication Data
Sadler, Wendy
Energy. – (Science in your life)
531.6
A full catalogue record for this book is available from the British Library.

Acknowledgements
Alamy Images pp. 24 (ImageState), 26 (oote boe), 16 (Phil Degginger), 22 (PHOTOTAKE Inc.); Corbis pp. 7 (Jose Luis Pelaez, Inc.), 25 (Julie Habel), 9 (Karl Weatherly), 4 (Ken Stralton), 13 (Lester Lefkowitz); Digital Vision pp. 12, 27; Getty Images pp. 23 (Brand X Pictures), 15 (Digital Vision), 5, 17, 18, 19, 29 (PhotoDisc); Harcourt Education Ltd pp. 20, 21; Harcourt Education Ltd pp. 14 (Trevor Clifford), 8, 10, 11 (Tudor Photography); Robert Harding p. 6 (John Miller).

Cover photograph of woman inline skating reproduced with permission of Getty/Stone.

Every effort has been made to contact copyright holders of any material reproduced in this book. Any omissions will be rectified in subsequent printings if notice is given to the publishers.

The paper used to print this book comes from sustainable resources.

An adult should supervise all of the activities in this book.

Contents

Any words appearing in the text in bold, **like this**, are explained in the glossary.

What is energy?

Energy makes things happen. Anything that you can see that is moving, hot, bright, noisy, or stretched has energy. Cars driving down the road, lights in your house, musical instruments, and rubber bands all use energy in some way.

Energy is all around us, all the time.

Energy in your life!

How many ways have you used energy in your life today?

- running around
- thinking – your brain uses energy!
- turning on a light
- kicking or throwing a ball
- stretching a rubber band
- listening to music
- watching television
- using a computer
- speaking to a friend on the telephone
- eating lunch.

A waterfall has lots of energy. Sometimes this energy can be used to make electricity.

All sorts of energy

There are lots of different types of energy. Light, **electricity**, heat, movement, and sound are all types of energy. Energy can be changed from one type to another.

A light bulb uses electrical energy and turns it into light and heat energy. A hot drink also has heat energy. Sometimes you can see the heat escaping as steam.

This hot drink will cool down because the heat energy is escaping into the air as steam.

Anything that moves has moving energy. This kind of energy is called **kinetic energy**. When you throw a ball, you give it some of your energy. When the ball moves through the air it has kinetic energy.

When you hit a ball with a bat you are turning your energy into kinetic energy to make the ball move.

Batteries are a useful way of carrying energy around with us. A battery has **chemical energy**. The energy comes from the chemicals inside the battery. Some batteries can change electricity into chemical energy and be used over and over again. These are called rechargeable batteries.

Hidden energy

There are other types of energy that you cannot see or hear. Sometimes things are not noisy, hot, or moving — but they can still have energy!

Energy in your life!

Take an elastic band and stretch it out. Now let it go. What happens?

A stretched elastic band has energy hidden inside. The energy came from you when you stretched the band out. The hidden energy is called **potential energy**.

Gravity is a **force** that pulls everything down towards the ground. If you lift a ball up off the ground you give the ball some hidden or potential energy. When you let the ball go it will fall back towards the ground. The potential energy has been turned into moving or **kinetic energy**.

A skier has potential energy at the top of a slope. This will turn into kinetic energy as the skier travels very fast down the slope!

Storing energy

Sometimes it is helpful to store energy so that it can be used later on. A spring is a simple way of storing energy.

If you squash a spring, it gets shorter than it wants to be. You give the spring energy when you squash it. The squashed spring stores this energy. When you let go of the spring, the stored energy pushes it back to the length it was before.

A spring can store your energy until you let it go!

A spring can be used to store energy in a wind-up alarm clock. When you turn the key at the back of the clock a spring inside the clock gets squashed. You are giving the spring energy as you do this. The spring unwinds slowly and releases the stored energy over a long period of time. This energy makes the clock hands turn to tell you the correct time.

What would happen without springs?

Without springs we might not be woken up in the morning!

This clock stores energy inside a spring.

Energy changes

Food contains **chemical energy**. Our bodies turn energy from food into heat energy, movement energy, and sound energy.

When you break food down in your stomach, your body turns the chemicals in food into other types of energy. This gives you the energy to run around and keep warm. Even when you are asleep your body needs energy to keep you alive.

We all get our energy from food.

A power station can use fuel, such as coal or oil, to make **electricity**. The fuel has chemical energy inside it.

When fuel burns it makes heat energy. The heat is used to boil water. The boiling water makes steam and the steam is used to turn a machine called a **generator**. The moving energy from the generator is turned into electrical energy for our homes.

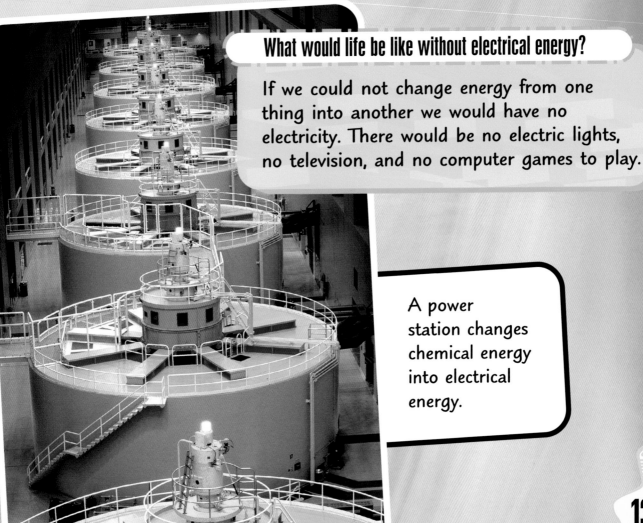

What would life be like without electrical energy?

If we could not change energy from one thing into another we would have no electricity. There would be no electric lights, no television, and no computer games to play.

A power station changes chemical energy into electrical energy.

Heat

Heat is a very important type of energy. It is the energy given out by tiny **particles** called **atoms**. Atoms are the building blocks of everything on Earth – even us!

When things have a lot of heat energy, tiny atoms are moving around very quickly. When things are cold, the atoms move more slowly.

The brakes on a bike turn moving energy into heat energy. The brakes rub against the side of the tyres and slow the wheels down. The energy from the moving wheels makes the brakes hot.

brakes

Our bodies must have the right amount of heat to work properly. If we get too hot or too cold we can become ill.

Humans are **warm-blooded** animals, which means that our bodies make heat energy from the food we eat. **Cold-blooded** animals do not make their own heat. The heat of their bodies depends on how hot or cold it is around them.

Lizards are cold-blooded animals. They have to sit in the sun for a while to get warm enough to move around.

Energy on the move

Energy often needs to be moved from one place to another. Oil that is used in power stations often has to travel from another part of the world. It is sometimes carried in pipes under the sea, or in large ships called tankers.

Gas is a form of energy we can use to cook with, or to heat up our homes. The gas travels to our homes through pipes.

Burning gas can make enough energy to heat food.

Electrical energy is made in power stations. This electrical energy is then moved across the countryside and into towns and cities. It moves along wires that are held up off the ground by huge **pylons**. The electricity is then sent into our houses along wires. The wires in your home are hidden inside the walls.

Electrical energy is moved around the country through wires like these.

When you carry your packed lunch from home to school you are using your energy to move the food. When you eat your lunch you will get energy from the food that you carried with you!

Nature's energy

Plants on Earth get energy from the Sun. Heat and light from the Sun help them to grow. Inside the leaves of a plant the Sun's energy is used to turn water and a gas called **carbon dioxide** into food for the plant. This food gives the plant the energy it needs to grow.

Animals eat plants and use the energy from the plants to move around, keep warm, and grow. Other animals may eat these animals, and they turn this food into the energy they need. Without the Sun's energy there would be no plants. Without plants there would be no animals.

Everything on Earth needs energy from the Sun to survive.

There are some machines that can turn energy from the Sun into electrical energy. These are called solar-powered machines. A solar cell or panel collects the energy and turns it into **electricity**.

Can you see the solar panel on this calculator? If you block the panel so that the light cannot reach it, then the calculator will not work.

Energy in our food

Our bodies need energy to work properly. We get our energy from food. If we have more energy than we can use then it is bad for us. Our bodies have to store this energy as fat. Too much fat can be unhealthy.

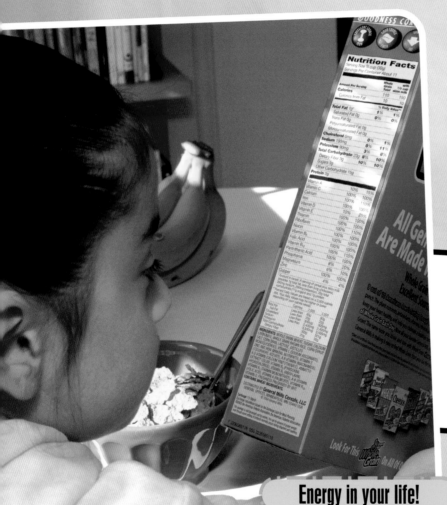

On food packets you can find out how much energy is inside your food. Look for the chart on the back of the packet.

The energy inside food is measured in kilojoules or calories. A high number means a lot of energy.

Energy in your life!

Collect some packets of your favourite foods. Find out which have the most energy and which have the least.

Foods that contain lots of oil or fat will contain lots of energy. Other foods, such as potatoes, pasta, rice, and bread also give you energy.

Fruit and vegetables contain less energy, but they contain lots of vitamins. Vitamins are just as important as energy. You should always try to eat a mix of different types of food to stay healthy.

Energy supplies

Most of the energy we use in our homes comes from burning oil, coal, or gas. The **electricity** in our homes comes from power stations, where these fuels are burned. Gas can be piped into our houses for heating and cooking.

Coal, oil, and gas are called **fossil fuels**. They are our most important energy supplies.

Oil is often found in rocks under the sea. Drills dig into these rocks and the oil is piped up to the surface.

One day in the future these fuels may run out. We need to use these precious supplies carefully. We should try to use less energy around the home. Can you think of ways to do this?

Another problem is that when fossil fuels are burned they give off a gas called **carbon dioxide**. This **pollutes** the air and can harm the environment.

Cars get energy from burning petrol or diesel, which come from oil.

Energy forever?

One day **fossil fuels** will run out. They also make a lot of **pollution**. Scientists are trying to find new ways to make **electricity** so that we do not need to burn so much fossil fuel.

Energy from the Sun, waves, wind, and the tides can be used to make electricity.

When the wind blows, the blades on these windmills turn around. The moving energy is turned into electrical energy.

In some countries people get energy from the Sun. They have solar panels on the roofs of their houses. These panels collect energy from the Sun and are used to heat water for the house.

Drying your clothes outside instead of in a machine will help to save energy.

Energy that will not run out is called **renewable energy**. This means that it will never run out. The Sun and the wind are both types of renewable energy.

Go easy on the energy

It is very important that we learn how to use energy carefully. Everybody can help to save energy. If we use less energy, there will be less **pollution**. The precious **fossil fuel** supplies will last a lot longer.

Think about all the things that you do that use electricity. What could you do to use less electricity?

We must all find ways to save energy. Everybody can help – and that includes you! How many ways of saving energy can you think of? Here are some ideas:

- put on more clothes when it is cold instead of turning up the heating
- walk or cycle to the shops instead of going in the car
- turn off lights when you go out of a room
- travel by bus or train instead of going in the car
- turn your television and stereo off when you are not using them.

Using bikes instead of cars can help to save fossil fuels.

Facts about energy

Energy is all around us. We use it for playing games, to stay warm, to give us **electricity**, and to travel places. But we must use energy carefully so that we do not run out!

Crayons, tyres, plastic bags, bubble gum, and deodorant are all made from **fossil fuels**.

The amount of **electrical** energy used by things around your home is measured in watts. Here are some examples of how much energy things use:

Electric oven	5,000 watts
Tumble dryer	5,000 watts
Microwave oven	1,500 watts
Fridge	200–700 watts
Television	55–90 watts
Laptop computer	45 watts
Clock radio	4 watts

You use twice as much energy when you are cycling as you do when you are walking!

You need to swim for about 20 minutes to use up the energy you get from a chocolate bar.

At the moment, more than 60 per cent of our energy comes from burning fossil fuels.

Find out more

You can find out more about science in everyday life by talking to your teacher or parents. Your local library will also have books that can help. You will find the answers to many of your questions in this book. If you want to know more, you can use other books and the Internet.

Books to read

Discovering Science: Energy, Rebecca Hunter (Raintree, 2003)

Science Answers: Forces and Motion, Chris Cooper (Heinemann Library, 2003)

Science Files: Heat and Energy, Steve Parker (Heinemann Library, 2004)

Using the Internet

Explore the Internet to find out more about energy. Try using a search engine such as www.yahooligans.com or www.internet4kids.com, and type in keywords such as "**fossil fuels**", "kilojoules", and "solar panels".

Glossary

atoms tiny particles that are inside everything

carbon dioxide gas that we breathe out, and plants breathe in

chemical energy energy that comes from chemicals. Food is chemical energy and batteries use chemical energy to make electricity.

cold-blooded animal that needs heat from the Sun to keep it warm

electricity form of energy that can be used to make things work. Computers and televisions work using electricity.

force push or pull

fossil fuels fuels such as coal, oil, and gas, which have been formed from dead plants and animals over millions of years

generator machine that turns movement into electricity

gravity force that pulls everything towards the centre of Earth

kinetic energy moving energy

particles very tiny pieces. Everything all around you is made up of particles.

pollution anything that is harmful to the environment

potential energy stored energy inside something that is lifted up or stretched out

pylon large metal tower that holds electric wires off the ground

renewable energy energy that will never run out

warm-blooded animal that can make enough heat to keep itself warm

Index